To my mother,

my husband,

and

my children, Genia and Danilo,

with love.

Copyright © 2013 Genia I. Nunez

Based on the poster The Cycle of The Seven Days of The Week/El Ciclo de los Siete Días de la Semana © 2000

English Translation & Edited by:
Genia D. Nunez Hernandez

www.genimpublishing.com

ISBN: 0991348524
ISBN-13: 978-0991348527
LCCN: 2013923833
Los Angeles, CA

All rights reserved. No part of this publication may be reproduced, stored in or introduced into a retrieval system, or transmitted in any form or by any means (electronic, mechanical, by photocopying, recording or otherwise) without the prior written permission of the publisher.

The Cycle of the Seven Days of the Week

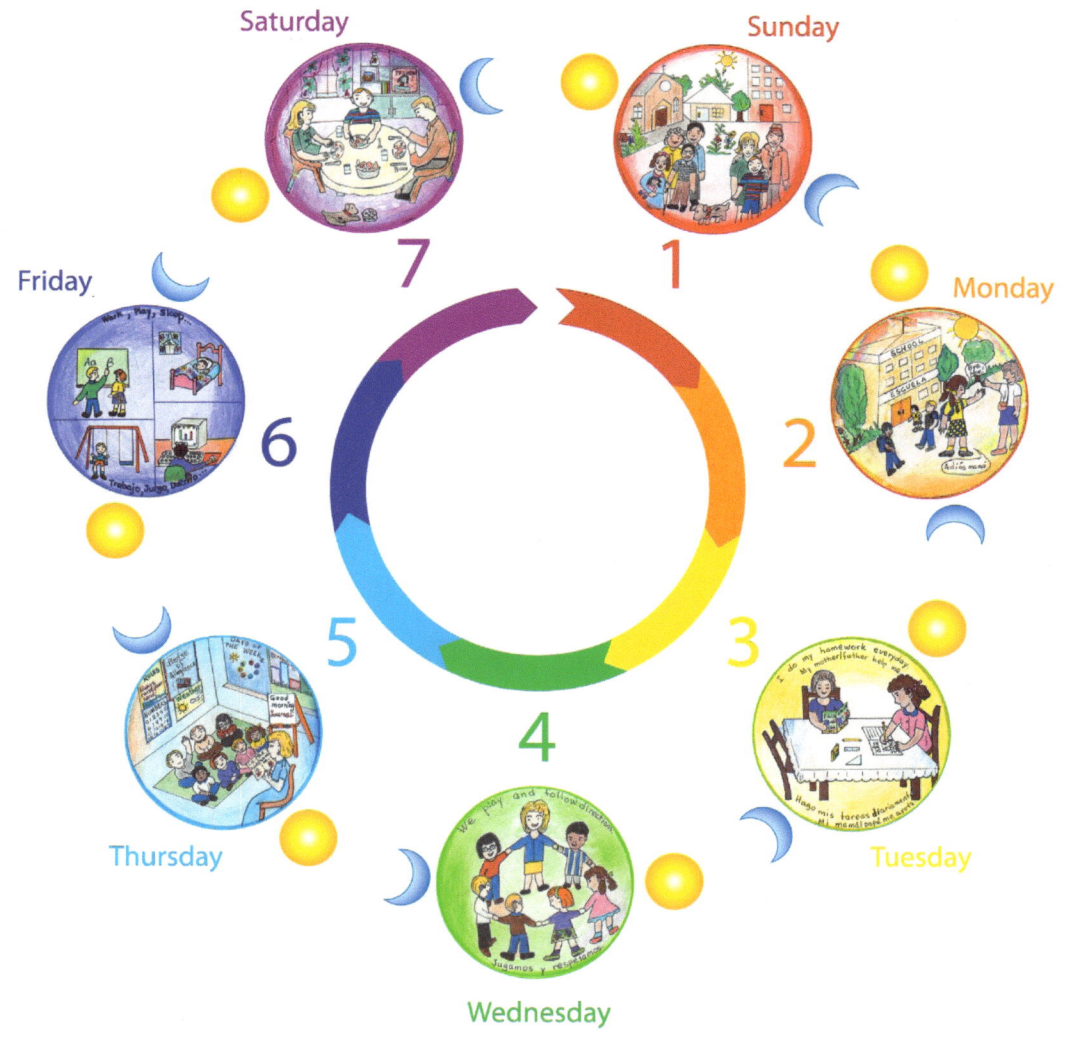

Genia I. Nunez

The sun comes out each day,
and each day will be filled with surprises.
Today's day can disappear as fast as a bubble!

Each day of the week is a gift to enjoy.
It's new and unique.
Even if we do similar things,
each day will be different.

Moon at night and sun at day.
It's a bright new day!
What day is today?

If we know what day it is,
we'll know what to do and what the day will bring.

The sun in the day and the moon in the night.
Day and night, night and day make the seven days of the week.

The seven days of the week form a cycle that repeats always in the same order.

Days of the Week

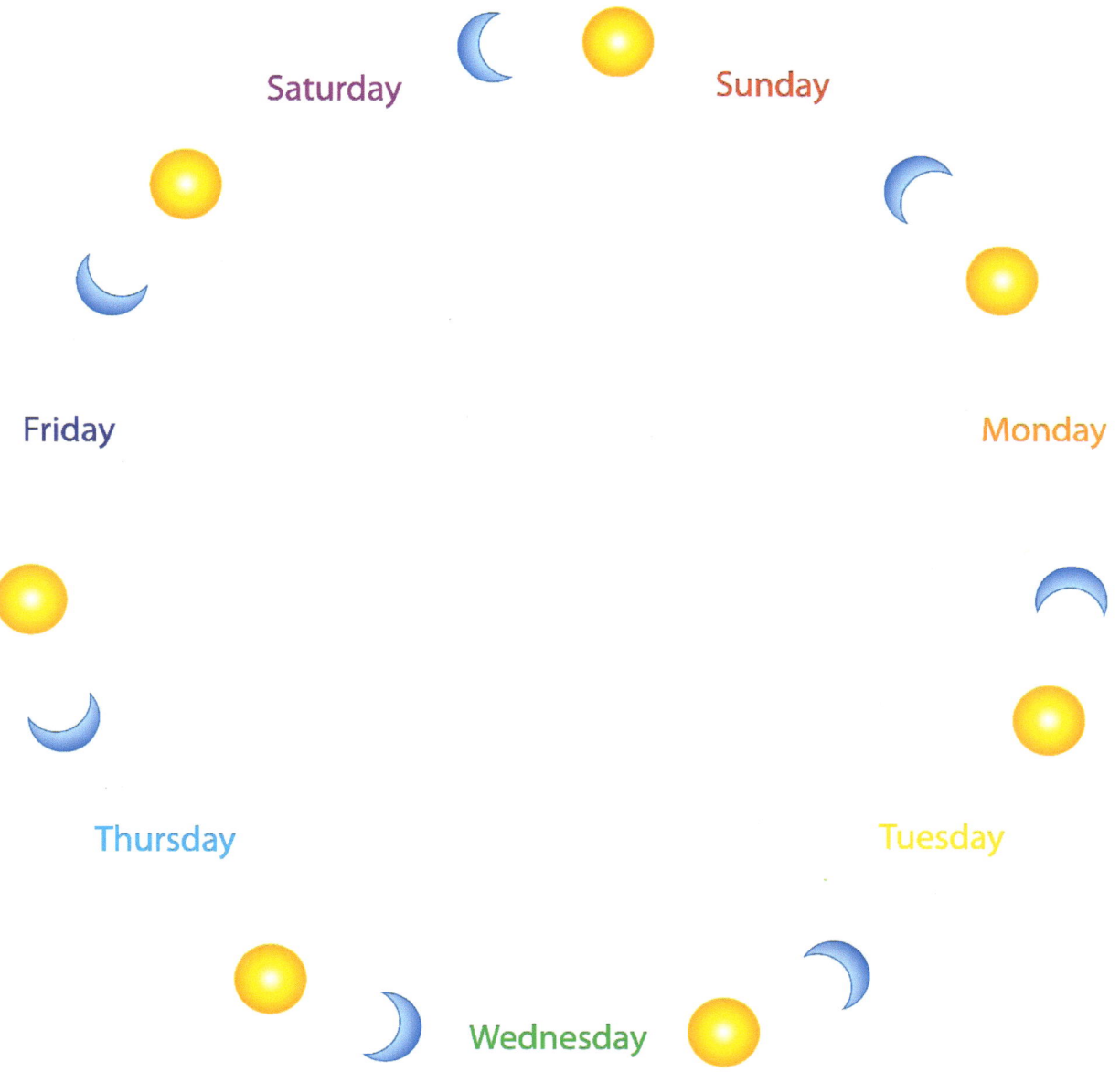

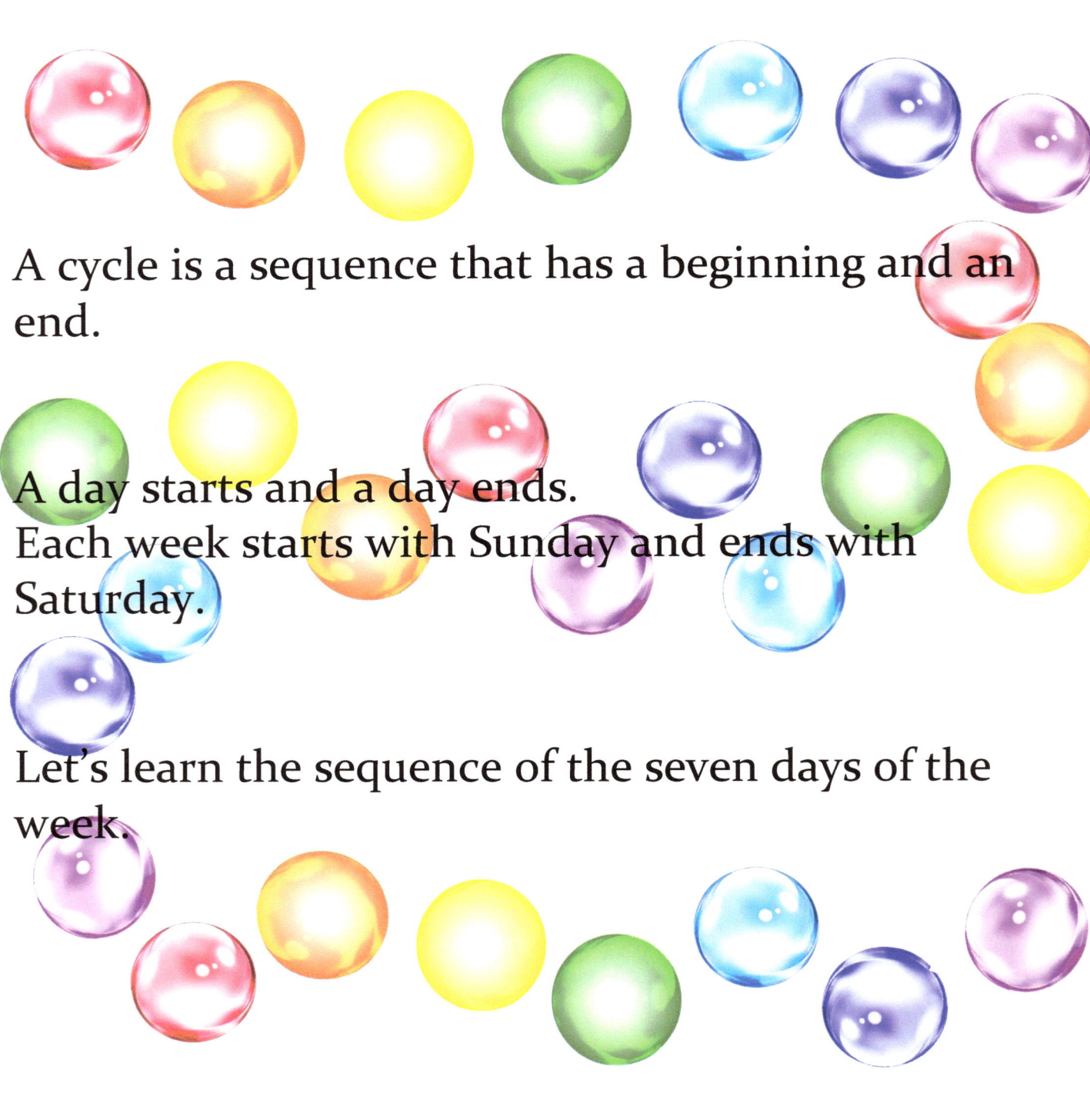

A cycle is a sequence that has a beginning and an end.

A day starts and a day ends.
Each week starts with Sunday and ends with Saturday.

Let's learn the sequence of the seven days of the week.

A Cycle of Seven

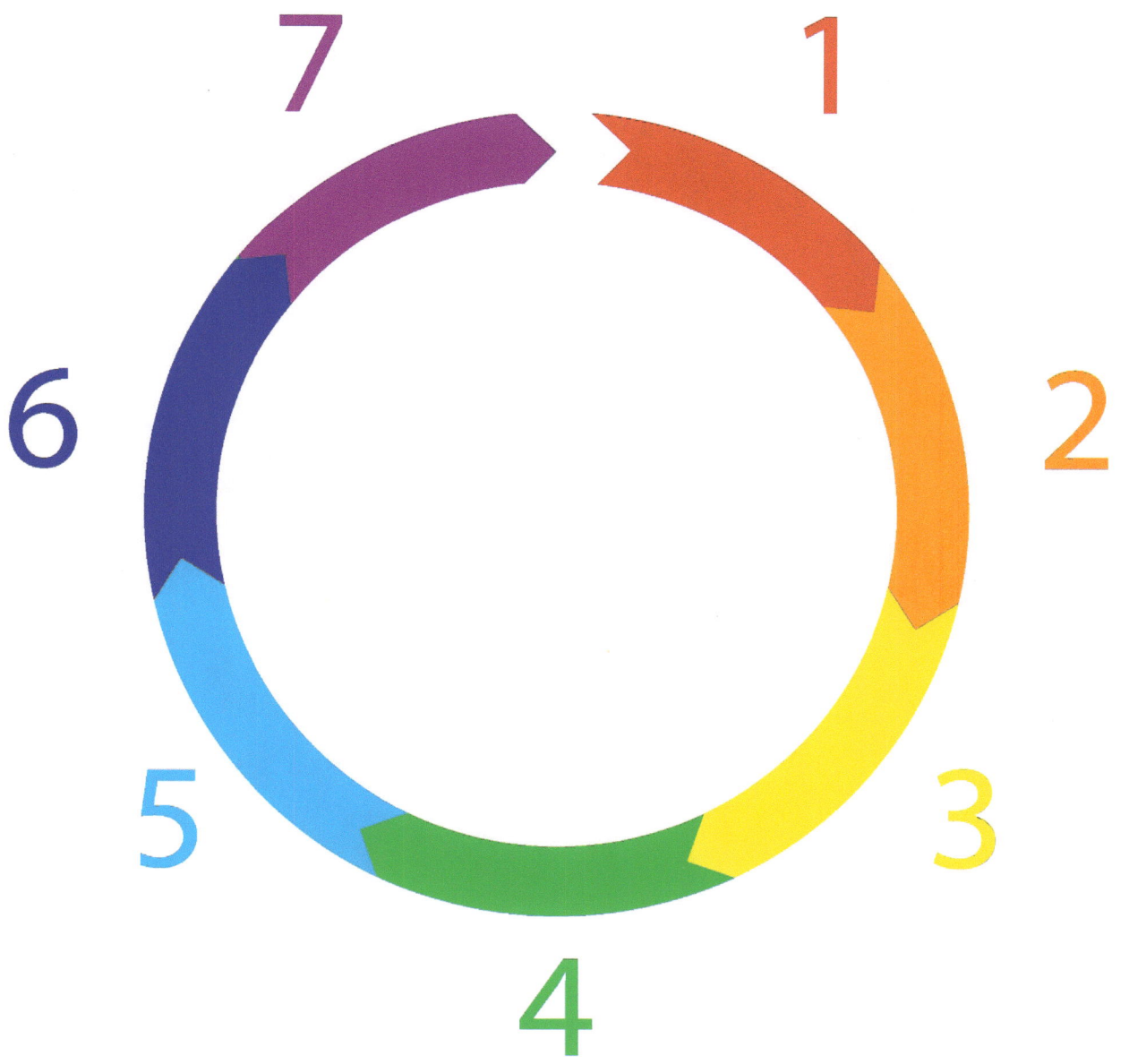

It's a beautiful day!
Today is **Sunday**, it's the first day of the week.

We share with our family,
we go to Church and meet with friends.

Tomorrow will be another day!

Sunday 1

Today is a new day.
It's **Monday**, the second day of the week.

It's the first day of school.
My mom takes me to school.

It's time to learn!

Monday 2

Another new day.
It's **Tuesday**, the third day of the week.

I wake up early, I eat my breakfast.
and go to school.

My homework is ready!

Tuesday 3

We're half way through the week!
Today is **Wednesday**, the fourth day of the week.

During recess we go out to the schoolyard.
We play together and have fun.

I like to share!

Wednesday 4

It's another brand new day!
Today is **Thursday**, it's the fifth day of the week.

The teacher helps us to learn the lesson
and reads us a story.

Reading and writing is fun!

Thursday 5

Again it's another day.
Today is **Friday**, it's the sixth day of the week.

We learn a lot in school doing different activities;
such as playing, drawing, reading and writing.

The weekend is very near!

Friday

6

A bright new day!
Today is **Saturday**, it is the seventh and last day of the week.

There is no class today, it's a day to rest.
I can watch TV, go to the park with my family and play my favorite sport.

Tomorrow will be **Sunday**.
A new week will start!

Saturday

7

Now I've learned the seven days of the week!

They are:

Sunday
Monday
Tuesday
Wednesday
Thursday
Friday
Saturday

Seven days are in a week to
work, learn, rest and have fun.
They're in a sequence day after day.

If I know what day is today,
I'll know what day tomorrow will be
and what day was yesterday.

The cycle of the seven days of the week
repeats week after week.

We just learned that seven days make a week.

Soon we will learn that four weeks make a month. Also, twelve months make a year which has it's own cycle.

And so on again and again!

A Week

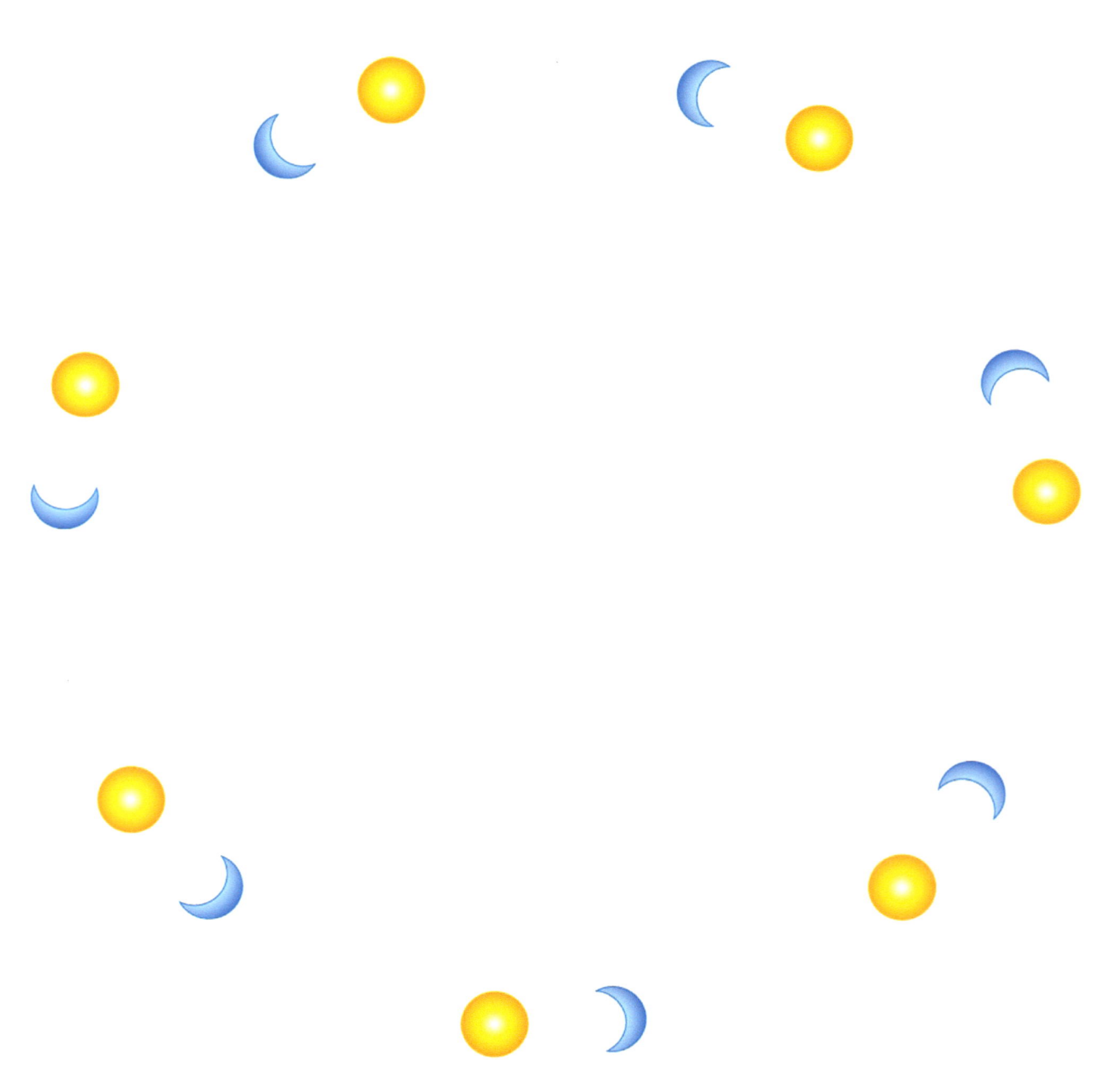

www.ingramcontent.com/pod-product-compliance
Lightning Source LLC
Chambersburg PA
CBHW041228040426
42444CB00002B/92